KU-241-044

Contents

How do your leadership skills shape up?

Answer these questions and work out your score, then read the guidance points overleaf for advice on how to boost your leadership skills.

In your mind, asking for advice is…

a) Unthinkable! Asking for help would be hinting that I'm incompetent.

b) I only ever ask others for help if I'm completely sure that I can't handle the situation in any way.

c) A good idea. You can always learn from others whatever your situation or abilities.

How much information do you give your team when you set them an objective?

a) Not much really: just the bare bones so that they can get the job done.

b) I like to set the scene a little, but if a job is urgent it's often simpler just to give them the objective and let them get on with it.

c) As much as possible. I feel that to motivate a team, you need to keep them informed and involved in what is going on.

To you, the idea of being in a position that requires you to give feedback to others is…

a) Scary! I wouldn't want to have to give someone negative feedback.
b) Not very appealing. I would try to avoid being too negative, maybe leaving out a couple of the mistakes in order to seem less picky.
c) Appealing. Helping people to improve their performance is a positive thing, even if some negative experiences or results have to be looked at.

Do you think successes within your team should be monitored and celebrated?

a) Not really, no. People get paid, don't they? What more do they want?
b) Yes, if the success is something extraordinary.
c) Absolutely. It's vital to celebrate a job well done: it will motivate the team to future success!

How do you feel about coaching someone?

a) As long as they learn to behave exactly as I do, that's fine.
b) I'd be glad to, but I worry that we'd talk about me more than them!
c) I think it's a great way to help someone talk through their aspirations and help them set some goals for the future.

Coping with change can be tough for managers. How would you work with colleagues who were fighting it?
a) I'd just lay the law down: they can always leave if they're that bothered.
b) I'd change my approach to suit them best. I'm uncomfortable with confrontation.
c) Initially, I'd listen more than I'd speak. You can't solve a problem unless you really know what it is, and it may be that the colleagues struggling with change have some valid points.

If your organisation is going through a turbulent time, what is the best way to 'steady the ship'?
a) It's probably best to ignore the situation until it becomes dire, surely?
b) Maybe it's best to make it sound worse than it is, so that any more positive result looks even better?
c) I'd try to stay optimistic, but honest.

Many managers today have to work with 'dispersed teams', whose members are based in different countries. How can you create a sense of team spirit in this case?
a) A cheery e-mail?
b) Regular teleconferences would help.
c) I think it's a good idea for the whole team to meet as soon as possible.

a = 1, b = 2, c = 3 Now add up your scores.

■ **8–14:** You may not feel as if you are a 'natural manager', but there is a lot you can do to boost your skills in the right direction. It's important that you remember that you have to take your team with you when you make decisions and plan their objectives, rather than simply imposing your views. Chapters 1 to 3 offer useful advice on the basics of good leadership, setting objectives, and improving your communication skills.

■ **15–19:** Once you've mastered the fundamentals of leadership, you can spread your wings a little and add extra skills to your repertoire. Coaching others is a growing part of being a good leader, for example, and chapter 4 explains how to do this well. As you grow in confidence, empower your team rather than hold all the power in. Turn to chapter 5 for help with this.

■ **20–24:** As you gain in experience, you'll be taking on more stretching tasks. For example, if the business you work for is having a tough time, it'll be up to you to help your team stay motivated and focused, as chapter 7 will show. If you're managing a dispersed team, chapter 8 offers advice and strategies for getting the most from everyone who reports to you — wherever they're based!

Developing your leadership skills

If you've just taken on a new leadership role, congratulations! This is a great step forward in your career. Part of being a good team leader is, of course, knowing how to inspire your team and take them with you as you strive to reach your goals. There are rafts of heavyweight management tomes about this very topic, but a lot of it boils down to common sense. In this chapter we'll discuss practical ways to help boost your confidence about this part of your job, whether you're relatively new to it or not.

There are many myths about leaders—'leaders are born and not made' being a prime example, and while it *is* true that some people are naturally better suited to leadership roles than others, the necessary skills can be learned, as you'll see throughout this book. It will help new managers get to grips with this aspect of their new job, and also help existing managers brush up on some new techniques and fulfil their potential. Good luck!

Step one: Understand that there are different types of leader

As you'd imagine, there are as many different types of leadership styles as there are people's personalities. For example, think of three shepherds.

- The first opens the gate and walks through, allowing the flock to follow—this shepherd **leads from the front**.
- Another stands behind the sheep and pushes or guides them through, demonstrating a **supportive leadership style**.
- The third moves from front to back and sometimes to the middle of the flock, demonstrating an **interactive leadership style**.

TOP TIP

Flexibility is key to good management. For leaders to exist, there must be followers, and the needs of followers change depending on the context. Knowing how to apply different leadership styles can help you respond equally effectively in many different kinds of situations.

Another school of thought recognises four leadership styles:

- directive
- process-led

- creative
- facilitative

Each one is related to a personality trait. Being more relaxed doesn't necessarily mean you can't be a leader—in fact, it's a positive boon in some circumstances—it just means that you have a natural tendency towards a certain type of leadership. As you become more confident and practised in leadership, you may be able to learn other styles—more dominant, intuitive, or structured, for example. Try to work *with* your preferred style until you are comfortable enough to branch out.

Clearly, certain styles are suited to particular situations. For example, a structured leader is likely to succeed in a situation where process is important, such as running a complex project. The relaxed or facilitative leader may be one who manages a professional group of people, while dominant leaders may be needed in businesses where there is a real drive or need for change.

Transferring your skills between different arenas

Don't worry if you feel more comfortable in some situations than you do in others—as you gain more experience and practice, you'll see that your skills really transfer across the different strands of your working life.

For example, let's say you can command an audience easily when you make presentations, but don't know if you'll be able to do the same with the team you've just started managing.

Commanding an audience is a great skill and many leaders have it, but it's not the sole requirement. Leaders also need to be problem-solvers and have originality and flair, confidence and self-knowledge, strong interpersonal skills, the ability to listen, vision, good organisational skills, and so on. Your ability as a speaker suggests that you're articulate and self-confident. If you possess the other qualities too, you're well on the way to being the leader your business needs.

Step two: Get some training

If the training budget in your business or organisation permits, a leadership course will help you gain a fuller understanding of what leadership is, and, by extension, how it will work for your business. Courses usually range from business theory to developing strategy and understanding business risk.

TOP TIP
Even if the benefits of some training are crystal-clear to you, it's no bad thing to spell them out clearly to your own boss when you ask to go on a course. A short e-mail explaining what you and the organisation stand to gain from it will show that

---

you're taking your new role seriously and that you're keen to take positive steps towards boosting your essential management skills. Try to appeal to your boss's pocket if you can; for example, find out whether you could get a discount for a group booking if other colleagues might also benefit from this type of training.

Having well-developed commercial awareness and a good business education will not only give you confidence, but will also help you command respect from others in the organisation.

Step three: Build self-awareness

Your leadership style is the means by which you communicate. The more self-aware you are, the more effectively it will work for you. This means knowing:

- what you are like
- what your preferences are
- what your goals are
- how you are motivated to achieve them
- how other people perceive you and your goals

Numerous tests and questionnaires can be used to help you explore your personality and preferences; they are widely available online as well as from books, consultancies, and other sources. Surveys are also useful and business schools have valuable data on expected leadership behaviours. You can combine information from all these sources to establish a benchmark for yourself.

Step four: Use it or lose it

Some leadership positions require you to set the objectives for others to follow. In these situations, scheduling, consultation, and the team building discussed in Chapter 2 are essential to success.

Leaders often need to work as intermediaries between two groups—those wanting the results (boards, investors, and so on), and those who will deliver the results. In this case you need to establish good communication channels with both parties that allow everyone to have the information they need at the right time.

The nature of the team you work with depends very much on your organisation and the type of work you do. You could, for example, work with one small 'core' team all the time, or you might need to build different teams for each different project you work on, selecting key people from across the business with the right skills to tackle the task at hand (these teams are often referred to as 'cross-functional').

If you need to put a team together from scratch, try to select a group of people that contains a good balance between competent managers and energetic, loyal team members. Teams need consistent, positive energy levels to sustain momentum, so it's critical that you choose a team based on the mix of talent required, rather than on friendships or office politics.

If you're trying out new systems or approaches, make sure you surround yourself with the right people, create a framework for support, and document the process so you can later evaluate what you have done.

TOP TIP
Leadership opportunities often crop up unexpectedly and if you work in a small business environment you'll come across them more frequently. As in most situations, your best bet is to start with an analysis of the situation. Decide what is needed, and how you can best achieve it.

The perils of the 'new broom' syndrome

If you're brand new to a leadership role, take it easy. While you'll be keen to get going in your new job and make your mark, tread carefully—at least to start with. Don't assume that your new team will welcome your style or your ideas with open arms, even if your predecessor was unpopular. They need to feel they can trust you and that you respect what they've been doing previously, before you can count on their support and co-operation.

Above all, don't depart too dramatically and quickly from established practice: even if you're desperate to change 'the way things are done around here', people are much less likely to throw up their hands in horror if you tackle things gradually. That doesn't mean that you do nothing, simply that you filter new ideas and ways of working bit by bit.

Step five: Lead by example

A good manager is also a role model, so it almost goes without saying that you'll have to set an example for how you want your team members to behave. Lead by involving people in establishing group objectives, setting standards, and achieving deadlines, and demonstrate your own strong personal commitment to achieving the team's goals. Set an example too by maintaining high standards in your appearance and general behaviour, and by establishing warm, friendly relationships.

Common mistakes

✗ You mirror other leaders too closely
People new to leadership roles may try to copy a leader they respect, because the person provides an easy model. This is understandable if you're feeling a little unsure of yourself in a new role, but you run the risk of creating a false impression of what you're *really* like, or, worse, making yourself look foolish for trying to mimic a

style that's incompatible with your own personality.
Good—and genuine—leadership comes from within.
Rather than follow someone else's style slavishly,
understand what it is that you respect in the other leader
and think about how you can best display that attribute.
If it doesn't work, don't be afraid to try a new approach.

✗ You don't work at it

Many people hope that they have natural leadership skills,
and accept leadership positions without proper training or
mental adjustment. This sink-or-swim approach works
sometimes, but not always! You're much more likely to be
successful if you build up leadership skills, increase your
self-awareness, and evaluate what you do.

✗ You make promises that may be difficult or impossible to keep

If you're a new manager, it's very tempting, during the
phase of settling in and relationship building, to make
all kinds of promises to your team, boss, or customers
in the interests of creating a good impression. Do
remember, though, that you'll be judged on whether or
not those promises are fulfilled, so be cautious about
what you say you'll deliver. It's much better to under-
promise and over-deliver than the other way round.

✗ You miss being friends with your team

This is probably the hardest part of promotion for many
people: you're thrilled at the great opportunity you've
earned, but know that your relationships with many
people will change irrevocably. Whether you're new to

the company or just the job, you need to build good relationships with your team members but also distance yourself a little from those who report to you so that you can be objective and unbiased in the way you work with them. This can be difficult when you've previously been a member of the team yourself, but if you don't, you run the danger of being seen as a manager who has 'favourites' and of allowing your personal feelings to affect your judgment. This won't be good for your team's morale and you'll also lose much of your authority. It's probably best to be honest about how you feel with particular friends so that you're seen to maintain a professional relationship at work, and you can then keep purely social activities for outside the office.

STEPS TO SUCCESS

✔ Try to be your own person. By all means observe good leaders in action and learn what you can from them, but don't mimic them. Be yourself, but get the training you need to take your skills to the next level.

✔ Remember the importance of context. There are many different management styles to suit a variety of occasions. Be flexible and be prepared to change your style depending on what you need to do and who you're working with at the time.

✔ Don't be afraid to ask for advice. We don't wake up in the morning instinctively knowing how to deal with every tricky situation we might come across at work, so do ask for help if you need it. Your manager, mentor, or a trusted colleague are good ports of call and their advice coupled with your own thoughts about how best to approach a situation will help you as you build your own 'brand' of leadership.

✔ Give yourself a chance. If you're new to a job or company, your first few months in a new role, especially one with management responsibilities, can be challenging. Don't get too downhearted if things don't go to plan: everyone makes mistakes. Reflect on what has happened, think about lessons to be learned, act on them as appropriate, and move on.

✔ Don't over-promise. It's tempting to get people on-side by telling them exactly what they want to hear, but you'll end up backing yourself into a corner.

✔ Tread carefully at first if you're introducing change. People's knee-jerk reaction to change tends to be negative, but if you bring it in gradually, you'll get a less panicky response.

✔ Lead by example. You can't expect others to behave professionally if you don't.

✔ Be very careful about what you say—and to whom— about your colleagues at work, even if they're driving you mad. Use your common sense and be discreet, however angry or upset you are.

Useful links

Management First (Emerald):

www.managementfirst.com/experts/leadership.htm

Entrepreneur.com:

www.entrepreneur.com

The Leadership Trust:

www.leadership.co.uk

University of Exeter, Centre for Leadership Development:

www.ex.ac.uk/leadership

2
Setting clear objectives

A key part of being an effective team leader is setting clear objectives from the outset so that you—and, most importantly, those reporting to you—can focus attention and energy on a concrete aim. This might be anything from a long-term career ambition that you've got to a small but vital task for a team member.

In fact, it doesn't really matter how big the objective is, as long as all the decisions you take and the activities you do are pointing in the same direction and leading towards the final target. So your team needs to know what's expected of them. Once you've all achieved your first couple of aims, you can start to set more ambitious objectives.

Step one: Ask yourself what's not working

I've set some clear objectives for members of my project team but they don't seem to be reaching them. They have all the resources they need. What's going wrong?

You may have set the objectives according to the needs of the project and forgotten that your team members need to be motivated and committed if they're going to meet them. Have you asked them how they'd like to contribute to the project and which objectives they'd like to take responsibility for? You may find that you've allocated the objectives to the 'wrong' people and that their interests and skills aren't aligned with your thinking. For example, it may be that the person you've asked to negotiate better terms with a supplier would be much more comfortable working on the new project visuals you asked for. If you invite feedback from your team about what they want to do, you stand a much better chance of allocating the best person to each particular task.

I know what objectives I need to set for my team so we can fulfil the company's needs, but I'm not being given timelines by my boss, even though I have (of course) asked for them. How can I motivate my team if I don't know how long we've got to get the job done?

Sometimes the information you need to set objectives won't be available to you. But you still need to try to pin down all the variables of an objective. You might have to guess the time horizon that you're likely to have to work towards or create your own timeline that will show your team in a good light. This means asking yourself what's the minimum amount of time that you've got. If you find yourself ahead of the game, think how you might reward your team for delivering the goods early so they remain motivated. Even though you've already broached this issue with your boss, keep on doing so until he or she gets the message.

I'm setting objectives for those who report to me and they're reaching them frequently, but they don't seem to be enthusiastic or energised by them. What can I do differently?

You may not be giving them sufficiently challenging or stretching objectives. If they're meeting your expectations too easily, they're likely to become bored and demotivated. Try asking them for their ideas about what they'd like to achieve. You may be surprised at their level of inventiveness and aspiration.

I find it hard to set objectives for myself because I don't know what I want to achieve in the future. How can I resolve this?

It sounds as though you haven't really discovered what motivates and inspires you in your current occupation. Think about what you've done in the past that's really excited you and ask yourself whether you can fold some elements of this into your personal objectives. Even if you find that what you're doing now isn't what you really want to do, you'll at least have focused your energy and discovered something about yourself. And that's one avenue you now won't have to go down on your quest to find out what you really want to achieve.

TOP TIP

Don't hold back! When you set an objective, you plant an image in your unconscious mind where it's lodged until it becomes reality. The good thing about the unconscious mind is that it isn't logical so it doesn't matter whether the objective 'makes sense' or not. The image will stay in your creative brain until your unconscious mind has succeeded in bringing it to fruition. This is how all creative people work—from inventors to artists, from architects to interior designers, from landscape gardeners to great chefs. They all bring 'concrete' form to the images they've seeded in their unconscious minds. You can make your ideas happen too!

Step two: Consider management by objectives (MBO)

Management by objectives, or MBO as it's more commonly known, is an approach to management that was conceived by business guru Peter Drucker in the mid-1950s. The underlying aim is to increase productivity and organisational effectiveness. It's largely disappeared in management circles today, partly because people are encouraged to short-circuit 'good practice' in order to achieve an objective. But the objective-setting part has endured and has re-emerged as an important way of focusing attention on what needs to be done.

Objective-setting is an important part of project management, which takes MBO a step further by incorporating and placing equal emphasis on the processes that lead to achieving a particular objective. It also caters for unexpected changes in the context or circumstances of the plan, as well as the impact of new information. Plus you have to remember human nature: how keen your team members are to reach the objective might vary from total disinterest to real passion for your chosen objective.

Step three: Set clear objectives the SMART way

On the basis that you need a goal or objective in order to achieve something, the notion of SMART objectives has survived MBO. SMART objectives are **S**pecific, **M**easurable, **A**chievable (or **A**ctionable), **R**ealistic (or **R**easonable, **R**elevant or **R**esult-orientated) and **T**ime-specific (or **T**ime-bound). Over the years, the acronym has acquired new words but the main aim is still to create order and process around objectives.

When you're setting an objective, or helping someone to set an objective, you might find it helpful to follow the SMART structure in sequence.

1 S (specific)
When you're setting an objective, it's vital that you're as clear as possible about what the outcome will look like. A

good question to ask yourself is 'How do you know when you've got there?' 'What does it look like?', 'What does it feel like?', 'How does it sound?', 'Is it mobile or static? Try to describe the objective in great detail. The more specific you can be at this stage, the more likely you'll reach the objective precisely. Try to focus on the ultimate form of the desired outcome. You'll find it's much easier to hold just one image in your brain than hundreds of confusing ideas!

2 M (measurable)

If your objective isn't tangible, as many aren't, you won't know If that you've succeeded unless you attach a measure to it. This may be a financial measure, a percentage or proportional measure, or a subjective measure, perhaps drawn from a survey of satisfaction. As long as you specify the measure at the outset, you'll know when you've achieved it.

Remember that if you set the measure incorrectly, and it's not directly correlated with your objective, you may find yourself measuring the wrong thing. If you want to get a sense of customer satisfaction for instance, and you choose the percentage increase in sales as the measure, you could find yourself thinking that you've achieved your objective when, in fact, there was a run on your product because your competitor ran out of stock!

3 A (achievable)

It's crucial that an objective is achievable otherwise you'll end up with a demoralised team. You need to reassure whoever's aiming to reach the target that what you're asking for is possible. However, the objective shouldn't be too easy. Setting targets that stretch people helps them gradually to improve in terms of quality, performance, productivity, and success. So, don't be too diffident when setting objectives. Add a bit of challenge to energise the people who're responsible for reaching them.

TOP TIP
Keep your objectives for others practical, factual, and tangible. So-called 'aspirational' objectives may have their place in career or personal-development plans but your ideas of aspirational objectives are very unlikely to motivate your team members.

---

4 R (realistic)

Remember that your objective must be credible in order to motivate someone to reach it. Being 'realistic' about the environment in which the objective has been set is helpful because it compels you to look at the obstacles or barriers that may sabotage your ability to reach the objective. Once this current reality has been properly appraised, you can start thinking of ways around it. If you pretend it doesn't exist, you'll be in for disappointment.

5 T (time-bound)

Setting a timescale enables you to create a process—and establish a rhythm. Knowing when to put in additional effort and knowing when you can take a rest is key. If you don't have a deadline, the chances are that some competing priority will emerge and your attention will be drawn from reaching your objective. Also, you may be responsible for an objective that's critical for another part of the process or plan. Any delay in your achievement could undermine the achievement of the overall goal.

If you use the SMART approach, remember that unless you attach personal motivation to the objective, the chances are it won't be met. Most people like to work in areas that have meaning for them and are often prepared to trade one less favourable objective for reward on a different level. But you need to have the prospect of the reward in place so that they'll take on responsibility and tackle the objective wholeheartedly.

TOP TIP

Some people see the world in a concrete and material form whilst others use more abstract and visual ways of interpreting their environment. When you're setting objectives, see if you can dovetail the nature of the objective with the style and approach of the person who's destined to achieve it. You could do this by asking them to explain how they see the objective and noticing the type of language they use, which you can then reflect back to them. In this way, they'll be owning the objective and will take responsibility for it.

Common mistakes

✗ You lose sight of what you want to achieve

Don't allow yourself to get bogged down in the variables and contingencies when you're setting objectives. Put all the variables and contingencies to a different part of your objective-setting activity. They may come in at the 'Realistic' stage where you identify what may get in your way.

✗ Reaching objectives becomes dull and routine

In operational environments, objectives are set and achieved all the time and may become routine and unexciting. If this is happening, try creating an overarching objective which everyone can work towards. This can add a bit of spice to what otherwise might be experienced as a repetitive and monochrome environment.

✗ You don't explain why you're setting an objective

Objectives are sometimes set in a vacuum with apparently no rationale behind them. 'Just do it!' is not an approach that breeds enthusiasm. Remember that people like to attach meaning to what they do and if they don't feel they're contributing to something valuable, they may not be motivated to do it, however essential it is. Even if you're under pressure, try to take time to place the objective in a wider context so that people can dock their efforts with something that they can believe in.

STEPS TO SUCCESS

✔ Don't fall into the trap of thinking that giving people objectives makes you a bossy leader. Your team members need to be focused on the task in hand and know what is expected of them. So it's up to you to point them in the right direction!

✔ Make sure you're matching the objective with the people skills available. Some team players may be better suited to one type of job than others.

✔ Work to a timeline—and if you haven't been given the overall timeframe then decide on a deadline that your team will be able to achieve.

✔ If your team seems to lack motivation, ask them for their ideas and what they want to achieve. Listen to what they say and set new objectives accordingly.

✔ If you're feeling uninspired at work, think about what you've enjoyed doing in the past and try to incorporate aspects of previous enjoyable jobs into your current role.

✔ Use the SMART acronym to help you set ordered and reasonable objectives for both yourself and your team members. Whatever you're aiming for, the ultimate objective should be Specific, Measurable, Achievable, Realistic and Time-bound.

Useful links

Job Search Manual—Setting Clear Objectives:
**www.jobsearchmanual.com/others/Setting_Clear
_Objectives.html**
The Practice of Leadership—Setting SMART Objectives:
**www.thepracticeofleadership.net/2006/03/11/
setting-smart-objectives**

3

Giving and receiving feedback positively

As part of your new job, you'll need to get to grips with the idea of *giving* feedback to others on their performance—normally as part of a performance appraisal—as well as receiving it about your own. Most people dread even the idea of it and assume that the experience will be a negative and uncomfortable one.

It doesn't have to be like that, though—feedback is, in fact, a gift. If you're giving feedback, your main motivation is usually to see people change their behaviour for the better, or to help them make the most of their potential. Feedback is rarely given maliciously and it can genuinely help others understand how they're perceived and how they can make positive changes to influence those perceptions. Perceptions are, of course, not always reality, but they're very real in their consequences, so being aware of these will help people choose whether or not to perpetuate them.

This is something to bear in mind when you're receiving feedback yourself. In the early days of a new job you can feel a bit beleaguered and not as confident as usual, so you may be more likely to take well-meaning advice as criticism. Keep your perspective, though, and listen carefully to what is being said rather than having a knee-jerk reaction and imagining you'll never get it right: it's likely that there is lots of constructive advice you can take.

Step one: Understand the benefits

Giving and receiving feedback is one of many forms of communication that goes on every day at work. One of the reasons that it's so unappealing is that, unlike a lot of the abstract, theoretical, or downright useless information we may encounter at work, feedback is essentially extremely personal and, as a result, highly relevant to the recipient.

Unfortunately, many people feel that the most common type of feedback they receive is critical. Sadly we rarely receive as much praise as we do criticism, even though we know that someone receiving lots of positive encouragement performs much more effectively than those who are constantly put down.

As part of your own objectives in your new role, you'll be doing yourself and your team a big favour if you can encourage in everyone a positive attitude towards the sharing of feedback. It is, without doubt, a challenge to do this, but remember that:

- feedback is a useful way of letting people know how they're experienced and perceived by others
- it gives recipients an opportunity to take decisions about whether or not they wish to change their behaviour and the consequences of doing that

Step two: Give feedback constructively

There's no way round it: giving feedback just isn't easy. If you've been on the receiving end of badly thought-out or tactless feedback yourself, the very thought of it may conjure up bad memories, and if it's an area with which you're unfamiliar or uncomfortable, a feedback session can easily spiral into a critical and defensive exchange rather than be a positive and illuminating experience.

There are plenty of ways to make sure that the feedback session you're in charge of does remain positive and constructive, though. For example:

✔ **Find an appropriate venue.** Make sure that the feedback session is held in a private place and that you can speak to the recipient without being distracted or interrupted. If you have an office, turn your phone on to voicemail or ask someone to field your calls, and remember to turn off your mobile phone or BlackBerry.

✔ **Make sure you're prepared.** Don't go 'cold' into feedback sessions of any type; it's not fair on the reviewee and is likely to increase any tensions that may be there. Check that you've collected all the information you need, and that you've thought through what you'd like to discuss during the meeting.

✔ **Make sure the reviewee is prepared.** If you're conducting a performance review, brief the reviewee so he or she has clear expectations on what will be taking place. Even if the reviewee has had an appraisal within the business before, it never hurts to run over timings and boundaries—some organisations prefer to hold performance appraisals and salary review meetings separately, for example.

TOP TIP
Some organisations have a standard form that all employees use to help themselves and their managers prepare for a performance review. These can include questions such as 'What do you see as your main achievements in the past year?', 'What are your personal objectives for the next twelve months?', and 'How could your manager help you more?'. Not all of these questions are pertinent to every organisation, clearly, but they may be a good starting point for your discussion.

✔ **Be positive.** Start off the session with some praise that shows you've noticed and valued particular behaviour. Remember not to use a one-size-fits-all approach in feedback sessions; you may have quite a range of personalities in the team you manage, so naturally you'll need a range of approaches to suit each person's personality. That doesn't mean that you can't address an issue directly, just that you need to make sure you broach it in the right way for the person you're talking to at that moment.

✔ **Focus on behaviour, not personality.** Make sure that any feedback you give focuses on behaviour (that is, something that can be changed) rather than on someone's character. For example, it's much more useful to ask someone if they're happy in their current position than to tell them abruptly that they're not pulling their weight! Always acknowledge a positive achievement first, so that the person you're talking to doesn't feel attacked. You can then have a discussion about what's going on, what you'd like to see happen to resolve it, and how you might help to make that happen.

TOP TIP

It's a good idea to find out whether the reviewee is willing to receive your feedback before you attempt to give it. If you think you feel defensiveness at the outset, address it directly. 'I sense that you're uncomfortable with this process. Is there anything I can do to make it easier for you?' You might want to add some reassurances also such as 'Any comments we make today will stay within the confines of this room'.

✔ **Take responsibility.** As part of your new role, remember to speak for yourself only. Use 'I. . .'

statements rather than hiding behind the views of a colleague or group.

✔ **Ask for feedback on the way you handled the feedback session.** Even if the session was difficult, it's an opportunity to build bridges and show your willingness to learn.

✔ **Honour any agreements made during the meeting.** If you've promised some additional resources, greater involvement in a project, or some training, confirm this afterwards in writing and follow it through.

TOP TIP
Always make a point of demonstrating yourself the behaviour you wish to see from others. It's no good asking for something from others that you're not prepared to do yourself. You can't expect people to speak to you openly about issues that concern them if you are impatient, defensive, or obstructive at every turn.

Listen!

Sometimes when you are nervous about something, you become so focused on what you want to say that you don't pay enough attention to what is being said to you. This can cause all manner of problems, including knee-jerk reactions to problems that aren't really there but which you *think* you've heard. If you're nervous about giving feedback to others as part of your new job, you'll benefit greatly from practising 'active listening'. This is a technique which will improve your general communication skills but which is particularly useful when you need to absorb and react to what others are saying to you in potentially tense situations.

Active listening involves:

■ concentrating on what is being said, rather than using the time to think of a retort of your own.

■ acknowledging what is being said by your body language. This can include keeping good eye contact and nodding.

■ emphasising that you are listening by summarising your understanding of what has been said and checking that this is what the communicator intended to convey.

■ empathising with the communicator's situation. Empathy is about being able to put yourself in the other person's shoes and imagine what things are like from their perspective.

■ offering interpretations and perceptions to help move the communication forward, then listening for agreement or disagreement. This enables both parties to start exploring the territory more openly. It is important to listen *for* at this point, which enables you to remain open to new ideas and to think positively about the other's input. Listening *against* results in you closing down to new information and automatically seeking arguments as to why something won't work.

■ questioning and probing which will bring forth more information and clear up any misunderstandings about what is being said.

■ not being afraid of silence. We often feel compelled to fill silences, even when we don't really have anything to say—yet silence can be helpful in creating the space to gather thoughts and prepare for our next contribution to the discussion.

Step three: Receive feedback positively

However much experience you have of working life, the prospect of getting feedback about the way you do your job can be nerve-wracking. The way we act reflects who we are to the world and when this is criticised or questioned, it can feel like an assault on our personalities. If you receive feedback that you find challenging or hard to deal with, try to put it into perspective—work is just one part of your life—and see it as information that allows you to make informed choices about how you're perceived by others.

In some circumstances, of course, the feedback (or the manner of it) may say more about the person communicating it to you than it does about you, but whether this is the case or not the best thing to do is to thank the person for their feedback and assure them that you'll think about it further.

TOP TIP

Do remember that you're not compelled to accept the feedback you get from others; it is, at the end of the day, their view on things. You can, of course, choose to carry on as you've been acting before, but do try to be pragmatic and see if it might be useful to bear in mind *some* elements of the feedback, even if other parts of it just don't chime with you at all.

Remember the following when you're receiving feedback:

- **Listen carefully.** Even if you feel under attack, try not to leap to your own defence until you've had a chance to think about and understand the feedback thoroughly. Be genuinely open to hearing what the other person is saying and try not to interrupt or jump to conclusions. The active-listening techniques discussed above may be helpful to you here.

- **Ask questions to clarify what's being said and why.** You are completely entitled to ask for specific examples and instances of the types of behaviour that are at the root of the feedback. Let's say that the person you're speaking to thinks that you should be more vocal in meetings. So you can adjust your approach best, ask him or her to tell you when they felt you needed to put yourself forward more. If the atmosphere is becoming tense, introduce a more positive approach by asking for examples of the behaviour they'd like to see more of.

■ **Keep calm.** Even if you feel upset, try not to enter into an argument there and then; just accept what's being said and deal with your emotions another time and in another place. Stay calm and focus on the rest of the feedback.

TOP TIP

As outlined above, giving feedback can be an uncomfortable experience too and people generally don't do it unless they feel that you can benefit from their observations. Try to remain engaged throughout and don't start a 'tit for tat' exchange.

Receiving feedback doesn't mean that you can't talk to the other person about your behaviour. For example, you may want to ask if the giver has any suggestions about what you could do differently or explain why you did things in a certain way at a certain time—the person you're speaking to may not be aware of all the pressures you were under at the time, or of the background to the issue at hand. You don't have to accept what the other person says, but asking for suggestions from them demonstrates a willingness on your part to take the feedback seriously. Round off the session by thanking the person giving you feedback for taking the time and trouble to share their perceptions with you.

Step four: Think about ways to improve the process

Honest and well-presented feedback allows people to enjoy good, open relationships. If feedback is a common feature of the way people communicate, issues aren't left to fester and grow out of all proportion—as they often can in a pressurised work environment.

Some organisations have benefited from nurturing a culture of 'instant constructive feedback' which encourages employees to address issues as they crop up, rather than to leave them to fester or develop into full-blown crises. This approach not only takes the heat out of more destructive or passive–aggressive styles of relating to others, but it can have a genuine impact on profitability as ideas may be freely exchanged and innovative approaches discussed. If you think this would be appropriate for your workplace, why not suggest it to your own manager or raise it with your team?

Common mistakes

✗ Both parties get defensive

As people can often feel under attack in a feedback session, they can become defensive. This often happens when either or both parties believe they are right and identify strongly with their 'cause'. As a result, people are unreceptive to suggestions about ways to work differently, however useful they might be. Tense situations of this type are difficult for most people to cope with, never mind someone new to a management position, but the best thing you can do is to keep calm and to try to maintain good rapport throughout. This involves the free expression of views and a genuine desire to understand each other's perspectives.

If you hit a rough patch, take a step back for a moment and quickly summarise what you've covered and agreed on so far: this will highlight the positives and hopefully lead to more constructive discussion.

✗ You make assumptions

Jumping to conclusions about other people's values, motivations, or intentions can quickly cause relationships to deteriorate. Rather than wading in armed with only your assumptions, give the other person the chance to explain how they've been acting or feeling early in the feedback session. Ask open questions and be patient: some people take a while to 'warm up' and feel comfortable in this type of setting.

STEPS TO SUCCESS

✔ Giving and receiving feedback doesn't have to be an uncomfortable or tense experience. See feedback for what it is: a useful way of showing people how they're experienced and perceived by others.

✔ If you're giving feedback to others, allow yourself plenty of time to prepare. Remember to:
- find an appropriate venue
- make sure the reviewee is prepared and knows the scope of your discussion
- be positive, and start the session off with some praise
- focus on behaviour (which can be changed) rather than personality (which is unlikely to!)
- take responsibility for what you're saying
- be sure to follow up on any agreements made in the meeting

✔ Make use of 'active listening' techniques. These will make sure that you concentrate on what is being said, rather than just wait for an opportunity to speak again yourself.

✔ When you're receiving feedback yourself, try not to take it personally. Work is just one part of your life and feedback is very rarely given maliciously. Remember to:
- listen carefully
- ask questions to clarify what is being said if you're not sure about it
- ask for specific examples so that you can see how you can do things differently next time
- keep calm, even if you feel upset; you're under no obligation to accept the feedback given to you, although it's wise to be pragmatic and to see if any (even if not all) of the points raised are useful.

Useful links

The ACTIVE REVIEWING guide:
http:reviewing.co.uk/archives/art/3_9.htm
Giving and Receiving Feedback, mapnp.org:
www.mapnp.org/library/commskls/feedback/
feedback.htm
Selfhelpmagazine.com:
www.selfhelpmagazine.com/articles/growth/
feedback.html

Coaching others

Business coaching is on the up—and if you're able to coach those who report to you, you'll find that they'll work more effectively and will respond better to you as their leader. As in the sporting world, coaching in business has become associated with helping people to channel their talent and achieve their full potential.

Effective coaching brings many benefits: not only does the financial investment return many-fold, but productivity rates also rise; the ability to make thoughtful decisions increases; and motivation improves. Also, there are often marked behavioural shifts in those being coached. As you become aware of your style and impact, you'll find that you're able to communicate more honestly and more easily. Constructive feedback, active listening, and unambiguous language all contribute to a coachee's repertoire of relationship-building tools which, when focused on the business, can increase creativity and innovation and add real bottom-line value. This chapter will show you how to be an effective coach!

Step one: Learn to ask the right questions — and to listen

You don't need expert knowledge to be a good coach, but you'll find it easier if you've a general understanding of interpersonal relationships. And you do need to be interested in helping others to develop their talent. Above all, you must be able to ask good questions, and to listen carefully to the responses you get.

The point of coaching is to ask questions that prompt someone to voice their innate knowledge, thoughts, concerns, and so on. As the people you're coaching reveal what's on their mind, they're bringing out into the open things that would otherwise have remained hidden. This allows them to make concrete decisions based on a clearly articulated, well-reasoned understanding of the issues. By taking self-responsibility in this way, coachees are releasing their own talent, not mimicking someone else's. In essence, when you're coaching someone, you're offering them the means by which they can hear themselves think (and talk) through an issue or aspiration.

Step two: Let the person you're coaching come up with the answers

Before long, your coachees will probably propose something that's been tried unsuccessfully before. But it's important that you don't just dismiss their ideas out of hand. Sometimes, to save time and money, you might have to steer someone towards a different course of action. However, coaching becomes much more effective when coachees discover for themselves what does and doesn't work. If you ask them what the likely barriers to success are and how they'll get around these, they may find themselves arguing against their own original idea! Being told that something won't work is very dismissive and de-motivating. Try to spend your time *questioning* rather than *telling*.

Step three: Make time to coach your team

You may think that you've got enough problems meeting your own work agenda and that you can't possibly find a spare half hour to coach anyone else. But it's a fallacy that good coaching takes time. Often, if you ask just one or two well-positioned questions, they'll trigger a series of thoughts that leads to a positive outcome. If your coachees are part of your team and you develop a coaching management style, you should find that the burden of your responsibilities is eased as they take a greater share of the workload.

Coaching doesn't have to be formal—sometimes, people don't even know they're being coached! But if you're taking a more formal route, before you move into the coaching conversation, you need to set the context. What's the situation you're discussing and what are the

circumstances of your conversation? Make sure you won't
be disturbed by people or phones and check you've left a
reasonable amount of time. You won't be listening properly
if you have to keep an eye on your watch!

The GROW model

If you're planning a formal coaching session, you may
find it useful to base the conversation on the GROW
model—one of the commonest approaches to coaching.

The model guides coaches in their conversations with
those they are coaching with an elegant logic that takes the
coaching conversation from *defining* the goal to *planning*
how that goal will be reached. It's based on asking good
questions, listening carefully to the responses, reflecting
these back to the coachee, and giving feedback.

GROW stands for:

- **G: G**oals
- **R: R**eality
- **O: O**ptions
- **W:** the **W**ill, the **W**ay, and the **W**rap-up

The individual stages are as follows:

Goals

First, you need to agree and set the goals. These must be
SMART goals: **S**pecific, **M**easurable, **A**chievable, **R**ealistic,
and **T**ime-bound (see Chapter 2). It's not worth setting
goals that can be reached without effort so try to set goals

which will stretch your coachees and maximise their development and experience.

In order to pin down these goals, you'll need to use open, probing questions (ie questions that start with 'Who. . .?', 'What. . .?', 'Where. . .?', 'How. . .?', or 'Why. . .?'). Open questions encourage coachees to speak at length, and to explore their inner selves. If you're looking for a 'yes'/'no' response, you'll limit the discussion's potential for discovery.

The following questions are designed to open up the discussion and to help your coachees agree on a SMART goal that will stretch them. These are only suggestions— you'll need to adapt them to your own style and words so that they feel right when you're asking them!

- What would you like to achieve from this coaching session?
- What's the aim of this discussion?
- Can you tell me how you see your goal?
- What are your aspirations?
- What do you think you need to achieve on the way to fulfilling your aspirations?
- Can you describe to me what outcomes you'd like to see?
- What are the SMART goals you want to achieve—in the short, medium, and long term?
- Why are you hoping to achieve this goal?
- How will you know when you've achieved your goal?
- How do you think you'll feel once you reach your goal?

Reality

Once you've established the goal, you'll need to do a reality check. You need to create what could be called 'structural tension' between where your coachees are *now* and where they wish to be in the *future*. You might think of this tension as a stretched rubber band. When you relax the rubber band the two ends come closer together, just as when you resolve the tension between the goal and current reality, the goal comes closer.

You could ask the following questions:

- What is happening now?
- What obstacles or barriers do you see on your path to reach your goal?
- Who is directly or indirectly affected by the pursuit of your goal?
- Are there any critical relationships you need to cultivate?
- What challenges do you think you'll encounter on the way?
- What will help or hinder you in the achievement of your goal?
- Who might help you, and who might hinder you?
- What does your intuition tell you to do?
- What assumptions are you making? Can you challenge these?

This reality check is not meant to be negative; it's simply realistic, with the aim of distinguishing the 'beginning' from the 'end'. This is why it may include some seemingly negative statements.

Options

Once you've fixed the beginning and end points, you can invite your coachees to brainstorm the options. This is where they can explore the possibilities and opportunities available. As this stage is about coming up with ideas, encourage your coachees to think the unthinkable and contemplate the 'impossible'. Even the most off-the-wall ideas can trigger a series of thoughts that brings a new understanding of the issues and may reveal a unique path through.

You could ask the following questions:

- What options are available to help you reach your goal?
- What have you considered so far? And what have you discounted?
- Are there any opportunities that you could use to your advantage?
- Do you see any alternatives to your preferred approach?
- Can you think of any novel approaches to assist you?
- What would happen if you did nothing?
- What would be your ideal solution? (Break some rules. Be outrageous!)
- Are there any cost constraints?
- Do you have any more ideas?
- If a miracle happened, what would it look like?

The Will, the Way, and the Wrap-up

This final stage is about choosing an option and building an action plan. It's also about ensuring that your coachees are committed to achieving the goals that they've set. In this part of the conversation, ask them to:

1 outline the steps he or she will be taking
2 explain the contingency plan if these steps don't go according to plan
3 describe the resources that are necessary to reach the goal
4 set some milestones
5 describe what support will be needed along the way

At this stage you could ask:

- What's your immediate priority?
- What could you do as a first step?
- Are any of the steps dependent upon the success of a former step?
- If this doesn't go according to plan, what's your contingency?
- How committed are you to achieving this goal?
- What steps do you need to take to achieve this goal?
- When are you going to start taking action?
- What support and resources do you need?
- On a scale of 1–10, rank your level of determination to achieve your goal. (If less than 7, you're unlikely to do it!)
- How would you summarise (or bullet-point) your final plan?

TOP TIP

Throughout any coaching conversation, you'll need to show excellent listening skills. This means suspending judgement, disbelief, and your own agenda as well as disciplining yourself not to jump to conclusions, interrupt, or finish your coachees'

sentences for them. It also means clarifying your
assumptions and confirming your understanding
with each coachee. Although this sounds
cumbersome, active listening is an excellent skill
to develop. When combined with positive body
language and a clear intention, you'll find that the
trust and rapport you build will ease the coaching
process—and any other conversations and
negotiations, business or otherwise.

Common mistakes

**✗ You don't see the value of asking open
questions**

This is often the case with new coaches, who can end
up giving in to the temptation of telling the coachee
about their own expertise and experience. Sessions
where the coach gives guidance and advice to the
coachee achieve nothing but a regurgitation of what's
happened in the past, regardless of whether things
have moved on. Try to discipline yourself to continue to
ask questions that will enable the coachees themselves
to work out the best way forward.

**✗ You allow time pressures to get in the way of
good coaching**

Sometimes, when particularly pressed for time, you'll
have to issue an instruction rather than work through the
coaching process described above. When this happens,
make sure you go back and review what's happened

and why. In this way coachees can learn retrospectively, and next time they'll be able to apply that knowledge.

✗ You try to form your coachee in your own image

Coaching isn't about creating clones, but about tapping into the creativity and latent knowledge of another person in order to find a new perspective on a situation. Try to be open-minded, and enjoy discovering the idiosyncrasies of someone else's thoughts and suggestions. Research has linked good coaching practice to increases in innovation, productivity, and bottom-line results. The rewards are there to be enjoyed by everyone.

✗ You tell stories about your own experiences

It's always tempting to tell 'war stories' instead of mining for other people's inventive ideas. Try to keep your ego out of the coaching conversation. Coaching is not about you; it's about building someone else's professional capability and credibility. Your glory will come when your coachees begin to deliver excellent results regularly.

STEPS TO SUCCESS

✔ When you're coaching, ask open questions (that invite more than the answer 'yes' or 'no') and practise active listening. Apart from when you're asking questions or giving your coachees feedback, try to keep quiet and let them do all the talking.

✔ Try not to be dismissive of new ideas, even when you know they won't work. Let your team-members come up with their own solutions and answers questions themselves.

✔ Make time for coaching your staff—that way, you'll find you're quickly working with a more productive, enthusiastic, and motivated team.

✔ If you're having a formal coaching session, set aside a time and place for the conversation so that you won't be disturbed. Use the GROW model as a framework, and encourage coachees to set their own SMART goals.

Useful links

Management Consulting News: Coaching ROI: 'Wow' Your Clients with Real Results:
www.managementconsultingnews.com/articles/ battley_coaching_roi.php
12 Manage Rigor and Relevance: Management Methods, Models and more:
www.12manage.com/methods_coaching.html
Mind Tools: The GROW Model: Coaching team members to improve performance:
www.mindtools.com/pages/article/newLDR_89.htm

5 Empowering your team

The word 'empowerment' has received a lot of bad press in the business world. To many people, it's 'the dreaded E-word!' This is possibly because 'empowerment' has been used so often to appease discontent, and as a means of abdicating responsibility—if managers can get employees to adopt a sense of ownership and power, their own load becomes less onerous!

But if you want to be an effective leader, you need to realise that, in essence, empowerment is a good thing. Research shows that empowered individuals experience improved initiative, energy, and motivation. Their self-confidence is increased, as is the level of tenacity they display when faced with setbacks. Empowered staff take responsibility for making decisions and following them through to completion. They feel energised and excited by what they're doing and are prepared to commit to achieving mutually agreed goals.

Imagine what an organisation would feel like if every employee were empowered. If you can visualise that potential success, you'll get an idea of how much disempowerment currently

exists in modern organisational structures. That's why you need to empower your team. Read on to find out how to do this while staying fundamentally in control.

Step one: Know the business benefits of empowerment

In today's current business environment, many things are unknown, untried, and unexpected. An ideas-based economy isn't predictable: problems appear out of the blue, and you can't always be clairvoyant and anticipate what your competitors are going to do!

Less-confident (and less-empowered) employees usually feel ill equipped to deal with this constant ambiguity, so you'll have to encourage them to take responsibility and manage their way through uncertainty. By tapping into their ingenuity, curiosity, and spontaneity, employees can approach business challenges in their own way, rather than waiting to be told by you what to do, how, and when.

Some managers find empowerment and delegation threatening but as a leader, you need to make use of every vestige of enterprise available to the business. To do this, you must be able to adapt and move from being a governor to being a channel. If you ask your team members to contribute at all levels, everyone can add value and the business will benefit.

Step two: Create the vision and motivate your team colleagues

Before you can empower individuals, you need to harness their enthusiasm and creativity. This means painting a meaningful, positive picture for them of what the future could look like and how they could contribute to it. Even if it seems far-fetched, try to create a sense of being 'in this together' and invite people to add their efforts to the collective goal. If they 'accept' your invitation, you can maintain their commitment by giving them space to use their discretion and talent.

When you first try to empower members of your team, you may find it hard to get them to shed the dependency they have on being told what to do. To re-engage them with their work, you'll need to motivate them to contribute their brain- or brawn-power to your collective efforts. Otherwise, you'll have to carry the load on your own, which is bound to be pretty exhausting and demoralising. Try asking your colleagues what motivates and energises them and see whether you can entice them with something that takes into account where this interest and excitement lies.

Step three: Decide on how to start empowering those who report to you

First, you'll need to understand the values, goals, and motivations of the people who are key to your success.

Once you've identified their passions and what drives them, you can align this knowledge with what you feel needs to be done in the business. If you're unsure, ask your colleagues to share their aims and objectives, and to explain both what and how they wish to contribute in order to achieve this personal vision.

One of the best ways to empower your colleagues is by creating a coaching culture within your team. You could try using the GROW model (explained more fully in Chapter 4) as a framework for your coaching conversations:

- **G:** What is the **g**oal?
- **R:** What is the **r**eality? What point are you starting from?
- **O:** What are your **o**ptions? What ideas have you got to get you from R to G?
- **W:** Which **w**ay will you go? Which option will you choose and what is your plan to get you there?

Remember that effective delegation is another proven way to start opening up to empowerment, as it gives team members a chance to take responsibility and own a goal or objective for themselves.

Step four: Know when to control and when to let go

Once you've empowered your team, you may feel usurped and out of control. If you feel the need to redress the balance, you may need to remind them that your role is to set the team's course within the context of your organisational objectives. Praise them for their initiative, find some concrete examples of where this has made a real difference, encourage them to do more—and ask that they keep you in the loop so that you can add your steer to their activities. State the importance of needing to know what is going on so that you can represent their achievements to members of the senior executive team.

If you work in a technically specialised area where mistakes aren't an option, you might want to empower your team but find that they just aren't up for it, given the limited margin for error. If you suspect that they're giving up without trying, you may be controlling the team too much. Try giving them the resources they need to do their job and the discretion to use them in the way they feel is appropriate—within certain limits, of course. They may make a few mistakes but if they feel truly empowered, they'll take responsibility for dealing with these.

Step five: Root out any blockages

Organisations, unwittingly, often ask for one set of behaviours while systematically encouraging another. For instance, if an organisation wants to achieve its goals through teamwork, it's pointless having an incentive scheme that rewards individual achievement. Similarly, if an organisation wants to be known for its responsiveness to customers, it should abandon any rules that prevent members of the customer service team from using their initiative.

Have a look at the processes that exist in your business and check that there aren't any contradictory messages being sent out through the existing systems and processes. If there are, decide how to resolve the problem as soon as you can.

Step six: Provide encouragement and support

If you're going to empower people, you need to make sure they're properly supported. Ask yourself what resources are needed in terms of information, knowledge, and skills. You may think that members of your team or organisation have sufficient internal capability to make the transition to empowerment— but perhaps they could do with some concrete encouragement to help them.

Think about how you can support empowered behaviour and try to identify the existing channels of communication. Are these channels clear and free-flowing, or are they blocked by organisational politics or etiquette? You may need to be proactive in asking your team what they'd like you to do to help them to make the switch to empowered behaviour. You may also need to act as a sounding board so that any concerns, frustrations, and disappointments can be fielded and dealt with positively. You don't want them leaking into the social culture of the organisation as negative stories.

TOP TIP

Most people find behavioural change threatening.
They're being asked to do something that they've
never done before and they're likely to feel
exposed and vulnerable. They may be asking
themselves what will happen if they 'get it wrong'.
If things don't go according to plan, you'll need
to manage your response very carefully. It's
important not to deny the existence of problems,
but make sure you debrief colleagues properly, to
create a sense of positive learning rather than
of criticism.

Step seven: Monitor and celebrate success

When things go well and you see good examples of
empowered behaviour, make sure that they're rewarded
and celebrated. This will show your team members that
you're taking the change seriously and encourages more of
the same. Circulate any success stories so that they help
to build up an ongoing positive image of the business.

Empowering people doesn't necessarily stop at the office
door. Some companies make a play of empowering their
customers. Think of the 'self-service' revolution, the
helplines, and the choices that can be made on the
internet. Think of the products that have brought about

the mobile technology revolution and have enabled less naturally resourced or privileged countries to compete in the world economy. Of course, there are some people who think it's gone a step too far and that organisations are abdicating their responsibilities to customers, but each case is different.

Common Mistakes

✗ **You keep your team on too tight a rein**

Some managers fear losing control when they empower their teams and therefore keep them on a tight reign with very little discretion to make decisions when they meet new challenges. If this describes you, be careful that you're not creating a 'jobsworth' environment where team members rescind responsibility and say 'It's more than my job's worth to use my initiative and risk getting it wrong.' Try gathering your team together and rooting out these susceptibilities by getting them to share the challenges they've encountered and explaining how they would have preferred to have dealt with them.

✗ **You don't know when to get involved**

Knowing when to get involved and when to let go is a difficult call. Sometimes it's necessary to let people learn from their mistakes, even if you think you could have prevented them from happening. Perhaps you could intervene only in 'business-critical' situations and make sure you're there to debrief help the team take on board the lessons learned when the time comes.

✗ **You mistake 'empowerment' for a business goal**

The business goal remains the same. The tools and techniques required to reach it probably remain largely the same. 'Empowerment' is a management philosophy that must permeate the organisational culture if it's to be successful. Make sure it's present everywhere, from the contracts of employment to the level of autonomy given to each individual.

✗ **You see empowerment as an easy way out**

This isn't what it's about. Empowerment still requires interest and involvement. Although empowerment gives people a sense of ownership and autonomy, it's not a substitute for engagement from the managerial level. Try to use it as a positive means for instigating purposeful and fruitful conversations and actions between all your team members.

STEPS TO SUCCESS

✔ Don't forget that empowering your team is a good thing. Colleagues will be positive, motivated and that is bound to benefit the business.

✔ Many hands make light work—and if you ask your team members for suggestions and ideas, to make a real contribution to the combined effort, you may well be surprised with what they come up with.

✔ Think about how best to hand over more responsibility to your team. Creating a coaching culture, where you really listen to what is suggested, could well be the way forward.

✔ Check that your organisation is committed to empowerment and isn't sending out mixed messages to its employees or customers.

✔ Make sure you congratulate individuals and the team as a whole when things go right. Sometimes, acknowledgement, praise, and a few incentives are all the encouragement your team needs to go from being moderately OK to amazingly successful.

Useful link

HR.com (search for 'empowerment'):
www.hr.com

Managing change

Change, as the saying goes, is the only certainty—in this dynamic world the only inevitability is change. People generally seek constancy, so we're permanently in a state of trying to prevent, fighting against or adjusting to change. At best, we can end up with 'dynamic equilibrium' where the ebbs and flows of life don't actually result in radical change but allow us to plan ahead with a degree of confidence.

And yet there are a few people who thrive on change. These are the 'change agents' who lead societal, industrial, and organisational change or who change the physical and creative limits of human endeavour. Without such change agents our world would be static, unimaginative, and dull. Yet many people resist the changes and challenges that change agents bring because they trigger fears that (illusory) control will be lost and that things will only get worse.

So, there's a push and pull of dynamic equilibrium on all levels. Understanding and not being frightened of the elements of change are key to successful leadership. This chapter tells

**you what to expect and how to best to go about
implementing changes.**

Step one: Pave the way for change

**I have implemented a change programme which I
thought it was going well until I started to notice
people going back to the old ways of doing things.
What can I do to rescue the situation?**

When you're responsible for a change programme, you'll be
lucky if you don't come up against opposition. It's likely to
be especially unpopular if it involves the loss of jobs or the
relocation of employees. Don't forget that there's bound to
be a rationale for the changes you've been asked to make
and you need to get this message across to those who'll be
affected. Perhaps you could start by pointing out where the
problem lies. You may be able to canvas views on the topic
and show empathy as you receive people's opinions. Once
problems are out in the out in the open and you've identified
how people are feeling, you'll have started the process of
getting people receptive to the idea of change.

Step two: Implement a change programme

There are two well-established methods used to
understand and manage change processes and, if you're

responsible for implementing change, it'll help if you follow the basic principles of both of them. Things will also be less fraught if you're prepared for peoples' likely responses to a change programme!

The first method is that of Kurt Lewin (1890–1947), who's often referred to as the founder of social psychology and father of organisational development. His name is behind the discipline of group dynamics and action research and he's best known for his three-stage theory of change.

Lewin believed that for organisational, group or individual change to take place the total situation must be considered. It's no good just looking at the little bit that you're interested in because it's only through embracing factors in the broader environment, and internalising them, that change can occur. It's in the boundary zone, the place where the internal and external worlds meet, that you—the change agent—need to focus your attention.

Lewin divided the change process into three stages:

1 **Unfreezing.** In order for change to occur, first you have to challenge and dismantle the existing individual and/or group mindset. Individuals have a particular way of looking at the world. Their values and beliefs, assumptions, observations and experiences—as well as their genetic and formative influences—all go to make up their mindset. If this is rigid and impervious to external influences, they won't change. So you'll often

have to use influence and persuasion to help people to overcome the inertia of the status quo.

In addition, those that you're introducing change to will very often adopt a defensive position. They'll see change as a threat because they fear losing control and losing what they perceive to be certainty. Sometimes, you'll need to give them a shock to 'jumpstart' the process of change.

2 Changing. Once you've dismantled the individual or group mindset, and explained what the changes are, there'll be a period of chaos and confusion. Nothing will be as it was before and a new mindset won't yet been formed to replace the old one. People who dislike of change often intuitively understand that it's going to be a bumpy and uncomfortable ride. What used to make sense won't make sense any more. So, after the unfreezing stage, there'll be a period of thinking things through from a different vantage point, of challenging assumptions and beliefs, and of reviewing the way things are done and experienced.

3 Refreezing. You'll have successfully introduced fundamental change once everything's been thought through from first principles and everyone's adopted a new mindset. At this stage, you'll have done most of the hard work and you should find a new level of comfort as everything settles again underfoot. At the refreezing stage, new approaches become part of everyday life and absorbed into a routine ensuring that change has properly taken place—and remains so!

The second model of change is rooted in the grieving process. You'll see a similar reaction in those who are being made redundant as in those who've been bereaved. Elisabeth Kübler-Ross (1926–2004) came up with a five-stage model that illuminates the behavioural responses to loss or change, and knowing about these will help you cope with people's reactions to change.

The five stages are denial, anger, bargaining, depression, and acceptance:

1 **Stage 1: Denial** When change is thrust on an individual—in the case of grief, living without a loved one—denial is often the first response. Whether this is conscious or unconscious, it represents a refusal to accept that someone's died. It's a natural defence mechanism that protects against distress. Sometimes, people can get locked in or stuck at this stage when they're dealing with a traumatic event.

2 **Anger.** Individuals often get angry when change is imposed upon them and their life is deeply affected. This can also happen in the organisational setting: frustration and anger can erupt in response to an action or event that prevents individuals from remaining comfortable and continuing in the way they were. This anger's often directed at the person who represents the change, even if they themselves have been forced to action it. So if you're the change agent, be prepared! When you know this is just a natural human response, you'll be able to anticipate and dispel it in a creative

way. Usually, once people have expressed their anger, they'll continue moving though the change process.

3 Bargaining. In the grieving process, although it may seem illogical, knowing pretty much that death is final, the bereaved often attempt to bargain with what represents God to them. 'If I promise to be good, will you return my loved one to me?' Less surprising is this tendency in organisations when a downsizing initiative is announced. The Unions will do all they can to broker a deal that returns the situation to the way it was or to find an acceptable compromise.

4 Depression. Next, it's usual for a bereaved individual to go through a phase of depression. This is the beginning of accepting that an ending has taken place and that facing the future without a loved one is inevitable. It's a 'grounding' emotion that prepares people for grieving. However, it still has an element of emotional attachment to it and is backward facing. In organisational cultures, you'll see people behaving with an air of despondency and post-shock inertia.

5 Acceptance. Finally, acceptance releases the emotional attachment to the loss and a certain level of objectivity and rationality returns. Indeed, there may even be a few signals that someone is prepared to move away from the loss. In an organisational context, you might find that individuals are more proactive and positive about the new options available to them. Perhaps people want to become part of a new team. Or they might apply for a

training course, attend an outplacement programme, or
a start looking for a different position altogether.

TOP TIP
Even if you think you need rapid change for your
business to survive, don't forget the human factor.
You need to give people time to recognise the need
for change, to think through their part in it, and to get
behind you. Try to be patient. Explain the need for
change and outline the threats as graphically as you
like, then turn to the people in your business for
ideas about what they could do. If they feel they can
influence the plan for change, they may become
aligned to it more quickly.

Step three: Make the changes stick

Sometimes a change programme seems to be going well
and then people start going back to the old ways of doing
things. This is most likely to happen if you decided to make
the changes in a vacuum and didn't bring in people
enough to make the changes stick. Try opening up a
discussion to find out why it isn't working and what they'd
like to see done in order for them to make the change
objectives a reality. You may not have followed through with
appropriate training or offered a sufficiently robust support
structure to help everyone when things got confusing.
One way to avoid this in future might be to create a
'change team' and let others take responsibility for the
initiative.

If you're implementing a number of change initiatives in quick succession, you might find people get tired of responding to the call to change. People become 'change weary' very quickly, especially if the changes aren't sustained or don't make a difference. If you find this is the case, you've probably got a lot of confused and uncomfortable people in the organisation who are distracted from doing their jobs well. Try to give people a 'change holiday' while they integrate the changes that have already been made. Also, arrange some sort of forum where they can discuss the changes and encourage them to offer each other support.

Common mistakes

✗ You don't prepare your staff

Organisations often try to initiate change initiatives in response to a new or sudden threat. However, unless you've prepared people for the prospect of change, they'll lag behind you in their commitment. Explain the need to be responsive and make them aware that change may need to happen unexpectedly. If they recognise the need for change, they're more likely to respond quickly when the occasion arises.

✗ You assume everyone agrees change is necessary

Very often, people have strong and fixed views and if you suddenly change their world, they'll have strong and fixed views about that too. Most people dislike the disturbance that change brings, even if it's ultimately to their advantage. Take time to get their assumptions and beliefs on the table and create a forum for discussion. You'll find that peoples' views aren't swayed by your strength of argument but in discussion with their colleagues.

✗ You don't give people time to adjust

Not giving people enough time to adjust to change before another initiative is launched is a common problem. People need time to 'grieve' the loss of the former situation and to accept and settle into the new. According to Kurt Lewin, change only occurs when the new external environment has been internalised and integrated. This doesn't happen immediately.

Similarly, don't expect people to accept positive change any more easily accepted than negative change. Any change requires an adjustment. At some of life's most positive change points, confusion and depression ensues. This happens in the personal realm as well as the organisational realm. How many times have you heard people say 'the honeymoon period is over', possibly referring to the 'low' after the 'high' of a promotion. Expect the change process to be challenging whatever its nature.

STEPS TO SUCCESS

✔ Warn people that there's a need for change, so that when you start making announcements and putting the change programme in place, it doesn't come as too much of a shock. They need to be receptive to change before anything happens.

✓ Follow Kurt Lewin's three-stage theory of change and give people time to adjust their mindset and ways of working.

✓ Remember that reactions to change are similar to the grieving process. Be prepared for individuals to go through the five stages of denial, anger, bargaining, depression, and acceptance.

✓ If the changes aren't working properly, talk to your team members to find out why. Keep the communication channels open at all times and don't expect people to accept change overnight.

Useful links

BusinessBalls.com—change management:
www.businessballs.com/changemanagement.htm
Work911.com—managing change:
www.work911.com/managingchange

7
Motivating others during difficult times

'Difficult times' can stem from many different factors. Some may arise from factors over which you have no control: your industry may be going through a turbulent period, for example, or innovations in technology may mean that your products and services may not be as popular as they once were. On the other hand, the problems may be closer to home: if your staff are unhappy, progress is being squashed by a dithering management, or the board has reached an impasse over future strategy, the ship is bound to feel that it's going through stormy seas.

Whatever the root cause, if it's your job to lead people during a difficult time, it can be a real struggle keeping morale up and productivity high. However, as most managers will find themselves in this position at some point in their career, it's worth knowing the best way of getting yourself and your team through, and leading them out the other side. It can be done!

Step one: Try to remain optimistic but honest

If it's clear to you that the outlook is bleak, try to stay cheerful and optimistic, but don't overdo it. If you're in such dire straits, your team can't fail but be aware of the situation. There's also a danger that your enthusiasm could be construed as desperation.
Be candid: call a meeting and explain the bigger situation, then describe your team's importance and explain why you think you should all continue to work productively.

You may find yourself in a situation where wages have been frozen and training budgets are non-existent but you should still be able to motivate the team. Remember that, although it's a contributing factor, money isn't the be-all and end-all of a fulfilling job. Your team colleagues need to feel that they're contributing to something valuable, so make an effort to build a sense of community, and to convey the importance of your work to the organisation as a whole.

If people have to take on extra work after a spate of redundancies, first of all you need to tackle the inevitable drop in morale that comes after restructuring. People may be relieved to have 'missed the chop'—but they've still had a nasty shock, and will understandably be unsure about their future. Most likely there's a very good reason why they weren't made redundant, so you don't want to lose them.

Give them the opportunity to tell you about their feelings and fears, in a team meeting or one-on-one—whichever they'd prefer. Be flexible about reallocation of duties: one person may want to take on a certain responsibility that someone else doesn't want to go anywhere near. It's only by talking to your team that you can help them to feel empowered and happier about their situation. Think about offering yourself as a coach so that your team can develop the skills they need to succeed in their new challenges (see Chapter 4).

Step two: Make an effort to keep yourself motivated

Particularly if you're having to pass on bad news, or even make people redundant, it can be difficult to keep up your own spirits and remain positive about the future. This is even harder if you don't agree with corporate decisions that are being taken by those higher up the ladder. Try to recall those times when you felt highly motivated and see whether you can bring some of those tasks or activities into your current situation. Also, put the current challenge into a broader professional or career context and see it as an opportunity to develop some valuable skills. You might also try doing something outside work that gives you pleasure to remind yourself why you are doing all of this!

Step three: Understand motivational theories

There are several motivational theories, the most prominent of which, perhaps, is Abraham Maslow's hierarchy of needs. Maslow (1908–1970) is endorsed by others who agree with much of this theory. Frederick Herzberg (1923–2000) came up with a two-factor theory specifically to tackle the issue of job satisfaction. If you're familiar with these two theories, it'll help you understand why people become de-motivated and what you need to do to re-engage them with their work.

Maslow's hierarchy of needs focuses on human needs per se, and suggests that there are five levels of needs which need to be satisfied in strict succession. As one need is satisfied, the drive to satisfy it is lost and the next level becomes the motivating force.

- **Level 1**: Starting with the basics, humans need to have water, food and comfort. These are the physiological needs that drive existence and must be satisfied before the next level kicks in.

- **Level 2** focuses on safety and security and suggests that once someone's physiological needs are met they seek more stability and consistency. This enables them to put their roots down and settle into a more comfortable existence.

- **Level 3**, meeting social needs then begins to drive someone's activities. At this level, people look for friendship and a sense of belonging. Social circles evolve and people choose to be with others who share the same values and beliefs and with whom they are pleased to be identified with.

- **Level 4** begins to motivate once someone's located themselves within a social setting. At this point, the desire for self-respect and recognition emerges. People at this hierarchical level of needs begin to define themselves separately from those in their close circle and want to be appreciated for the unique contributions they make to their social environment.

- **Level 5** finally brings self-actualisation. In fact, Level 5 might more accurately be described as self-actualis*ing* because it's an ongoing life process where the expression of someone's full potential is the driving force. This is where individuals seek to become all they can be and fulfil what they perceive to be their life purpose.

If you consider Maslow's hierarchy of needs from an organisational perspective, you'll see that:

- Level 1 equates to the provision of a canteen, a comfortable place to work, and a salary.

- Level 2 are the longer-term benefits of employment such as private health insurance, a bonus, and a pension. If these factors are absent, employees won't be loyal to the organisation and go to work somewhere else where they can feel safe enough to put down some professional roots.

■ Level 3 suggests a community of people who share a set of values and beliefs and who are working towards the same ultimate goal. Doctors, lawyers, accountants, and other professions bring together people with the same desire to satisfy Level 3 needs.

■ Level 4 drives personal definition and success.

■ Level 5 enables the expression of personal truth and life purpose. This level is often interpreted as having a wider 'meaning' element, such as a philosophy or religious belief.

Herzberg's two-factor theory distinguishes between hygiene factors and motivators. The hygiene factors may be considered to map onto Levels1, 2, and 3 of Maslow's hierarchy of needs and in a work setting would include salary, job security, and status as well as feeling part of a social/professional community. The motivators, equivalent perhaps to Maslow's Levels 4 and 5, are likely to include higher levels of responsibility, challenging work, and personal recognition.

If you apply these theories in the workplace, you'll see that once the basic needs are met, difficult and challenging times can actually motivate people to contribute at a higher level.

Think about how you can meet people's basic needs so you can move them towards more challenging tasks that will motivate them during difficult times:

■ Have you managed to put the fundamentals in place? This includes salary, canteen, and good working conditions.

■ Is there a bonus, health-care, or pension scheme that will demonstrate organisational support and loyalty towards employees?

■ Do you provide the resources people need to do their jobs? This means equipment, budgets, training, and coaching.

■ Are roles well defined and structured within the organisational hierarchy? Do people know what they're supposed to do and what their level of authority is?

■ Are people organised into teams and do these teams have a sense of identity?

■ Are the two-way channels of communication effective? Do people have a place to go when they want to voice their worries and concerns, either individually or collectively?

■ Are there ways in which people can be creative/ innovative and make a personal contribution to organisational success?

- Are there ways in which you can recognise people's achievements visibly? Does everyone have an area of expertise that they're known and appreciated for?

- Is there a compelling vision or purpose for your organisation's existence?

If all these factors are in place, you'll have a much better chance of motivating people during difficult times because their basic needs will have been satisfied and they'll be ready to put their energy towards overcoming a new challenge. Indeed, it's often found that adversity breeds ingenuity, capability, and high levels of engagement. When overcome, it also brings great satisfaction and reward. If you can paint a picture of the importance that each team member plays in getting over the difficulty, whatever it is, and if you can provide the appropriate level of care, concern, and support, you'll succeed in your mission.

Common Mistakes

✗ You give a pessimistic and negative impression

It's very de-motivating and disheartening if a team leader or manager demonstrates doubt about being able to overcome a particular difficulty. So, keep a positive outlook and have faith in everyone's ability to work together effectively in times of trouble. If you're trying to lead people through a particularly challenging

time, think about what you'd need in a leader to keep
you motivated. Certainty and confidence, whilst being
caring and concerned, are some of the qualities you
might want to see displayed—along with practical
capability, of course!

✗ You're dishonest about the current situation
Pretending that the times aren't as challenging as they
appear is a mistake. People are much more effective at
reading between the lines than they're given credit for
and they'll know if you're holding something back. It's
much better to be honest about the challenges that
you're facing than to withhold information in a parental
fashion.

✗ You become over-dominating and demanding
Fear of losing control sometimes results in leaders
becoming authoritative and over-demanding. Although
they may think they're appearing strong and in
command of the situation, this behaviour doesn't
achieve high levels of motivation, rather the opposite.
Try to be honest about what's going on and establish a
good communication flow so that people can air their
concerns and be sure of an empathic ear.

Although empathy is good in times of difficulty, you need to
put a limit on how much you'll allow people to indulge in
negative thinking and in worrying about problems that may
not emerge. Appreciate their concerns and then try to turn
the conversation into something concrete and positive.
Encourage them to think about what they can do to make

the most of the situation and turn it to their and their colleagues' best advantage.

STEPS TO SUCCESS

✔ Do whatever you can to keep your team motivated. Try to keep a cheerful and positive attitude.

✔ Don't lie about the situation if things get really dire. Remind everyone how valuable they are within the organisation, and keep them in the picture.

✔ Think about Maslow's hierarchy of needs and Herzberg's hygiene and motivator factors. Make sure there are incentives in place so people will want to continue to work for you.

✔ Keep effective communication channels open. They need to be working both ways so management and employees can get messages across to each other.

Useful links

Power Link Dynamics—Self-help tips for professionals:
www.pldynamics.com/archived-self-help-tips–2.php
Motivation ABC:
www.motivation-abc.com

Managing a dispersed team

Effective teams are at the heart of all successful organisations, but in the last few years our perception of what a team actually is has changed. Traditionally, teams tackled projects that brought them together regularly in one place so that strategy, progress, and (ultimately) success could be monitored. The vast technological advances of the late 20th and early 21st centuries have meant that *virtual* teams—often based in different countries, and sometimes different time zones—can tap into the Internet and other communications tools to work together on projects with a global reach.

Clearly, the dynamic in a virtual (or dispersed) team will be radically different from the norm, and if you're leading one, you'll need to find new ways to help the team bond and cohere. Many of the principles of team leadership are still valid, however, and there are plenty of ways you can make your team harness its strength and capabilities.

Step one: Establish the team's objectives and responsibilities

When you're asked to lead a widely dispersed team, don't worry about the geographical challenges for now. Start by putting in place the measures that allow strong teams in any environment. Make sure that the team is absolutely clear about what its aims are, the roles that each team member is taking on, and what success will 'look like'.

Good, regular communication is an absolute must but it can be a nightmare to arrange if team members are in different time zones and possibly based across three continents. Sometimes, someone will just have to bite the bullet and put themselves out by getting up early or staying up late to take part in tele- or Web conference. At other times, you could ask trusted team members to take on the job of passing on messages from you to colleagues near them. If you go down this route, make sure everyone gets to take a turn so that there are no grumblings about preferential treatment!

Step two: Meet in person at the beginning of the project

Unlike most teams, the members won't have many opportunities to meet in person, so try to set up a physical meeting as soon as possible so that the team can begin to bond and understand the value that each person is bringing to the collective effort. Gathering everyone together as the project kicks off is a wonderful way to get the ball rolling. Not only does it give you an opportunity to explain the commercial context for the work to be done, as well as outlining priorities and deadlines, but everyone on the team can also buy into discussions about how they'll keep in touch and how often.

On a human level, just breaking the ice, putting faces to names and laying the foundations for a strong working relationship will get the project off to the best possible start. Be sure to schedule in these group meetings regularly to monitor progress and, at the end, to celebrate a successful outcome.

It'll also help if you create a team 'brand' at the outset of the team's life together, so that everyone knows what entity they belong to and can build trusted and committed relationships within it. You might be able to do this by organising a team bonding exercise specifically aimed at forming such trust and relationships.

Step three: Clarify your team's expectations

Making the 'rules' clear is something that the team leader should tackle early on, so that good practice is in place from the word go. The 'rules' should cover general housekeeping issues as well as team etiquette points, for example:

- decision-making and conflict management processes
- expectations around timelines and deadlines
- team etiquette—time keeping, frequency of (virtual) meeting attendance, managing interruptions, listening attentively, giving/receiving feedback, and mobile phone management.

Given the challenges inherent in managing a dispersed team, it's a good idea to let each person take a turn in 'hosting' a meeting, so that the same person or people aren't always put at a disadvantage by time differences.

Step four: Use the Internet to create a shared team 'space'

E-mails are a great way to keep in touch, but you could also set up a dedicated team site within your company intranet so that everyone can keep track of each other. Ask the team to check in one day a week (every Monday, say) and to add in details of holidays, meetings, trade fairs, or conferences so that you can see at a glance where everyone is should you need to call a meeting or get in touch individually. You could also use this communal space to store important documents or even set up a blog.

You might find it helpful to e-mail everyone with a daily, weekly or monthly update on progress (depending on the timescale of the project), so that they're kept up to date. Hoarding information when you're leading a dispersed team is a recipe for disaster. Tell everyone what's going on and make absolutely sure they're aware of any changes to the project specifications and objectives. Putting revised details on your team's Web space will mean that no one will miss out.

Step five: Adjust your style

Because meeting in person isn't easy to arrange, most of your communication will be done online, over e-mail, or on the telephone. In the case of the first two options, irony and jokes may not 'travel' well without the visual cues you'd normally be giving people face to face. They may also baffle team members whose first language isn't the same as yours. That doesn't mean that all communication must be bland, simply that you should write clearly and positively, and avoid too many idiomatic phrases or slang. Use emoticons —:)—to keep the tone upbeat or indicate the emotions behind statements.

Step six: Foster a strong team spirit and monitor performance

In a more conventional setting, you've plenty of informal ways to keep in touch with your team—at the photocopier, by the kettle, or in the canteen or local sandwich shop. When you're leading a virtual team, however, you obviously lose out on this spontaneity but still need to strive to make everyone feel valued. Make sure you plan some time into your schedule every week to call or e-mail each member of the team to ask how they are, what (if anything) you can do to help, and so on. Show them that you're interested in what they're doing and keep reminding them that you value their contribution.

Trust is a key part of all working relationships but is even more important in a virtual setting when you can't physically see or hear what people are doing. You need to have confidence that every individual member of your team will pull their weight. For this to happen, of course, you must be very clear about what you're expecting them to do and when. Set each person a measurable set of goals that you can monitor and review regularly. This last part is crucial: out of sight definitely isn't out of mind, so working in this unique way isn't an excuse for anyone in the team to take their foot off the accelerator.

Common Mistakes

✗ You don't communicate effectively

Whatever type of team you lead, strong communication skills are essential for success. Many managers fall down in this area, however, and the added layer of complexity that being in different parts of the country or on different continents adds can result in communication becoming weak or fragmented. Yes, it's a challenge to find a way through that suits everyone, but you must plug away at it. Less isn't more in this regard, so talk to your team as a whole and then as individuals, too, so that everyone feels that their contribution is valued.

STEPS TO SUCCESS

✔ Try to have a face-to-face meeting with all team members as early as possible, and introduce the team to each other too so they can build relationships and trust more effectively.

✔ Spell out what each person is responsible for and don't forget to specify the timescale and deadlines.

✔ Make good use of the Internet and use your company Intranet if it has one.

✔ Take care over your e-mails—it's all too easy to be misunderstood if you're trying to be ironic, and sometimes jokes don't 'travel' well.

✔ Remember to thank all your team members individually when a project comes to the end.

Useful link

Chartered Management Institute:
www.managers.org.uk

Index